FEBRUARY

Valentine
Surprise

For Temi, with love —C. D.

For my always valentine, Zoë —R. W. A.

Text copyright © 2008 by Corinne Demas
Illustrations copyright © 2008 by R. W. Alley

First published in the United States of America in 2008 by Walker Publishing Company, Inc.
Distributed to the trade by Holtzbrinck Publishers

For information about permission to reproduce selections from this book, write to
Permissions, Walker & Company, 175 Fifth Avenue, New York, New York 10010

Library of Congress Cataloging-in-Publication Data
Demas, Corinne.
Valentine surprise / Corinne Demas ; illustrated by R. W. Alley.
p.   cm.
Summary: A little girl tries to create the perfect heart-shaped valentine
for her mother on Valentine's Day.
ISBN-13: 978-0-8027-9664-6 • ISBN-10: 0-8027-9664-8
[1. Valentines—Fiction. 2. Valentine's Day—Fiction. 3. Mother and child—Fiction.]
I. Alley, R. W. (Robert W.), ill. II. Title.
PZ7.D39145Val 2008   [E]—dc22   2007020143

Typeset in Goudy Sans
The art for this book was created using pencil, watercolor, and gouache

Book design by Nicole Gastonguay

Visit Walker & Company's Web site at www.walkeryoungreaders.com

Printed in China
10 9 8 7 6 5 4 3 2 1

All papers used by Walker & Company are natural, recyclable products made from wood
grown in well-managed forests. The manufacturing processes conform to the environmental
regulations of the country of origin.

Valentine Surprise

Corinne Demas

Illustrations by R. W. Alley

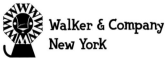

Walker & Company
New York

It was almost
Valentine's Day.

Lily wanted to make a valentine for Mommy.

She found some paper.
"I'll cut out a big heart," said Lily.
"It will be a secret until
Valentine's Day."

On Monday, Lily worked at her little table by the window.

She made a valentine.
But the heart was too **pointy**.
Puntiagudo

She hid it under her bed.

On Tuesday, Lily made a second valentine.

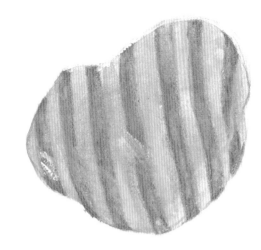

But the heart was too **round**.
redondo

On Wednesday, Lily made a third valentine.

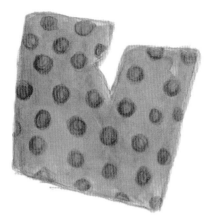

But the heart was too **square**.

Cuadrado

On Thursday, Lily
made a fourth valentine.

But the heart was too **curvy**.

...curvvoso

On Friday, Lily made a fifth valentine.

But the heart was too skinny.
flaco

On Saturday, Lily made a
sixth valentine.

But the heart was too **fat**.

gordo

Sunday was Valentine's Day.
Lily made a seventh valentine.
But the heart was **lopsided**.

desequilibrado

And she had used up all her paper.
Lily felt so sad. What was she going to do?

She had an idea!

Lily put out all the hearts on the
table and got to work.

A little while later, Mommy
came into the room.
"Happy Valentine's Day,
Sweetheart," she said.
And she gave Lily a
great, big hug.

"I tried to make you a valentine," said
Lily, "but it didn't turn out right."

Mommy looked at the cut-out hearts.
"Oh, Lily," she said. "I love you!
You made me a valentine for every
day of the week."

"But none of the hearts is perfect," said Lily.

"That doesn't matter," said Mommy.

"The heart inside you is."

And it was.